ANXIETY
The Fear, The Fight, The Freedom

SARAH BRYANT

Published by
Feather Pen Dreams
P.O. Box 8433
Green Bay, WI 54308

www.featherpendreams.com

ISBN: 978-0-9998563-0-7

FOREWORD

It's no secret that anxiety is running rampant in our society. We're often overloaded, overwhelmed and stressed to the max. Our minds can so easily be polluted with social media comparisons and nightly news reports of terror and division. We torment ourselves with endless thoughts of uncertainty like: Am I a good enough parent? Will I ever be successful in my career? Can I afford to pay the bills this month? Does my spouse still love me? What if I fail? Why am I even here? What's the point?

Maybe you can relate -- or know someone who can.

The good news is, although we face an enemy who wants nothing more than to see us minimized through fear and anxiety -- he is a defeated enemy thanks to Jesus. There is hope!

This is not only a beautiful story of one woman's journey of learning how to rest in God's love, but this book also includes systematic tools and steps to help you process through your own experiences and, ultimately, experience freedom from anxiety.

I pray Sarah's story would inspire yours and that your life's testimony would also be one of victory, peace, joy and rest, founded in God's promises.

Love and Blessings,
Beth Jones
The Basics With Beth TV

ACKNOWLEDGEMENTS

Thank you to my husband, Jared, for being a constant source of support and encouragement, both in my struggle with anxiety and in my struggle to write my story. Thank you for lovingly pushing me toward freedom and publishing my book.

Thank you to my daughters, Zoe, Rhema, and Olive, for your love and patience. Thank you for laying your sweet hands on me and praying that I would be healed. God answered your prayers.

Thank you to Erica Estrada and Chanel Penn for cheering me on throughout the writing process. Thank you, Erica, for your week-by-week writing accountability. Thank you, Chanel, for rallying a team to send me to writing classes. You both believed in me when I didn't believe in myself.

Thank you to Beth Jones for your support and guidance through the Inspired Author's Academy. You gave me the practical tools I needed to pursue my dream.

Thank you to Alyssa Arrington, creative genius, for

sharing your formatting and graphic design skills with me. The layout and cover design are stellar.

Thank you to Mindy von Atzigen for editing my book. Thank you for sharing your gift with me and giving my words the upgrade they needed.

Thank you to Jami McCain for dropping everything to be by my side when anxiety first hit. If anyone can make the ER a pleasant place to be, it's you. Thank you for making me laugh when I wanted to cry.

Thank you to Jamie Bryant and Tammy Chupp for taking the time to give me writing and publishing advice.

Thank you to Pastors Paul and Bonnie Booko for encouraging me to be healthy. You taught me that getting help when I need it is a good thing.

TABLE OF CONTENTS

PREFACE

A Letter to the Reader

What you are about to read is a story, my story, of my three-year battle with anxiety. My prayer for you is that reading through my story will provide you with the encouragement you need to begin your own journey to freedom. At the end of each chapter, there is some space for you to process the chapter and write your own thoughts, feelings, and experiences. Through your processing time, I believe that God will reveal to you your very own steps to a life free from the bondage of anxiety. If you feel like anxiety has a grip on you and you can't get out, this book is for you. You do not have to carry this weight around with you for the rest of your life. I thought I did, but now I'm free. You can be free, too.

Disclaimer: I am a human that was controlled by anxiety, and now I'm not. This makes me an overcomer who is encouraging you to become one, too. I am not a doctor! If you are considering foregoing medications that have been prescribed by a doctor, please consult with a doctor before making that decision. If you feel that your doctor does not listen to you, does not have your best interest in mind, or is more concerned with writing a prescription than helping you get better, I do suggest finding a different doctor. I found a great doctor who listens with the intent to really help and I believe that you can, too.

CHAPTER 1
What Is Happening To Me?

I was on my hands and knees in the living room of our small, two-bedroom apartment in Dallas. I was shaking, overcome by great fear and physical discomfort. My heart was pounding, it was hard for me to breathe, and I was sure something was very wrong with me. I had never experienced anything like this before.

The kids were at school, and my husband was preaching and ministering in another country. I dialed 911, but the line was busy. I called a second time...still busy. I didn't know that the 911 line could even be busy, but it was. I stood up and tried to walk, but I was extremely dizzy. I knew I needed to see a doctor, but I felt unable to drive myself, so I called a good friend of mine. She drove me to the closest emergency room. I walked into what was a packed house of people needing medical attention. I told the nurse I thought I was having a heart attack because that is the only way I knew to describe what I was experiencing. They let me go in right away and began testing me for heart issues. They then took me to a room to lie down and wait to see the doctor.

The doctor walked in with my chart. He was very

young, looking fresh out of medical school, with no stains or spots on his oversized, bright white lab coat. He sat down in front of me and proceeded to tell me that my heart was fine and he thought that what I was experiencing was anxiety. He explained that what happened to me that morning was a panic attack.

"I'm sorry, what?" I was completely taken aback. That was not the answer I was expecting. It had never even crossed my mind.

"Anxiety. I think that's what you have," he answered a second time. He handed me a printout explaining what anxiety was and a prescription for some medication to help me manage it for the time being. He then told me to follow up with my doctor for a more long-term plan. I left the emergency room with my friend, got my prescription filled, and headed home. I was in complete shock. I had never dealt with anxiety. I barely knew what it was. To be completely honest, when people would speak of having anxiety, I would think to myself, "Yeah, sure, I feel nervous sometimes, too. I think maybe they are overreacting." And here I was, dealing with something that I had once thought was exaggerated and sometimes even fabricated. At the time, we were living in a not-so-safe part of Dallas. In other words, if we heard sirens at night, it was a good thing because we knew the police were doing their job! I was very often afraid at night, especially when my husband was out of town, which was more often than not at this point in life. He was on two to three week mission trips pretty regularly, and I was in Dallas running the other details of our life and ministry.

We were raising two small children, running a missions organization, planting youth groups, and working other jobs. Our busy life was beginning to take its toll on me. Saying yes to nearly everyone and everything was catching up to me. And there I sat, alone, on our bed, in a small, two-bedroom apartment with a bottle of meds in my hand, wondering if I would be able to sleep, if I would be up all night, if I would even be ok at all.

I thought busy was good. I thought busy was noble, even. Yet, there I sat, broken and afraid, paralyzed by fear. My heart was racing, I found it painful to breathe, and even the slightest thought of something being wrong sent me straight into panic mode. I printed out some scriptures about fear and anxiety, took a half of a pill, and prayed to God that I could sleep. Or, if I couldn't sleep, that I would just be ok. Sleep was the goal, but I would settle for ok.

Sometimes, you don't realize something is wrong in your life until it catches up to you. Not only did my unhealthy lifestyle catch up to me, but it caught up to me so fast that it tackled me to the ground. Anxiety knocked me flat on my face. I thought I was doing the right thing. I thought that pushing myself to the edge and moving from one thing to the next to the next to the next was good, that it somehow made me worthy. I thought that accomplishing as much as possible could make me good enough for people and good enough for God.

I was so busy proving myself that I didn't realize I was ruining myself. Anytime I had anything nice or had a break or a vacation, I felt guilty. I didn't think I deserved to have fun or to rest; I thought I deserved to work, to earn my place in

> I WAS SO **BUSY** PROVING MYSELF THAT I DIDN'T REALIZE I WAS **RUINING** MYSELF.

the Kingdom of God.

I was discovering that I had been lied to all this time. My enemy, the devil, had convinced me that I had to work to earn a place in God's Kingdom, a place that I'd already been given. He knew that if I was busy enough, stressed enough, tired enough, and disappointed enough that he could convince me I would never have what it takes to be a child of God. He also knew I would be so busy that I would neglect caring for myself and getting the healing and everyday care I needed. I would be so busy ministering to others that I wouldn't get the ministry I myself so desperately needed. And he was almost right.

But, almost right is still wrong. Romans 8:28 tells us "that in all things God works for the good of those who love him, who have been called according to his purpose." Based on the truth of God's word, I knew that God could take my anxiety and use it for my good, to expose the enemy's lies and to introduce me to a whole new way of living that awaited me on the other side.

I wish I could say that it was an easy journey. I wish I could say that as soon as I discovered what was happening, it didn't happen anymore. Neither of those was the case for me. Shortly after my trip to the ER, I went to church and received prayer. The next week I felt amazing.

I thought it was gone, that I had been delivered and set free. I knew that God was capable of that. I had seen it in my own life in other areas and I had seen it in other people. Unfortunately, the anxiety was not gone and the panic attacks returned. I was entering what I didn't know would be a three-year-long battle with anxiety.

I would be driving to work and have the slightest little thought of possibly being a few minutes late, and sure enough, I would begin to panic. It was hard to breathe. I was terrified. I felt like I needed to escape, that maybe if I could run away, I could outrun it. I would have to pull over and breathe and take my medication and wait to calm down, praying that it would never happen again. I couldn't bear it happening again.

But, it did happen again, and again, and again. It began to negatively affect everything I did. It took its toil not just on my mind and my emotions, but on my body as well. Living with anxiety is like someone walking up behind you, catching you off guard, wrapping both of their hands around your neck, and squeezing until further notice, all the while leaving you wondering what on earth you did to deserve this kind of treatment.

If I were in a restaurant I felt was too good for me, I would get so nervous I would be unable to eat. If I were with people I felt were too important for me, I would become so anxious I would have to leave the room. I started having extreme headaches and severe stomach pain on a consistent basis. I was mentally and physically sick. I had to find out why this was happening to me.

THE ANXIETY LEFT UNATTENDED DIDN'T GO AWAY, IT ONLY GREW AND TOOK ON OTHER FORMS.

But, I couldn't figure out why I was having panic attacks. It was something I heard about happening to other people, not something I ever thought I would face. I was doing everything I knew to live right, so why was something so wrong taking over my life? It didn't make sense to me. It didn't add up.

Over the next year, I entered a coping phase. If I can just get through the panic attacks and pray for them to go away, then maybe one day that's what will happen. They came so unexpectedly, maybe they would just leave that way. And in a sense, that's what happened, or so I thought. I stopped having panic attacks for a short while, but the anxiety was still there, and it got much worse. The anxiety left unattended didn't go away, it only grew and took on other forms. Instead of slowing down my life, caring for myself, and looking for answers, I kept attending to all of my responsibilities, as if I could handle everything, just like I had always done.

What started as a panic attack on the way to work grew into an inability to eat whenever I felt like I didn't belong. Whether it was a birthday dinner in a fancy restaurant with my husband, or lunch out with co-workers I found intimidating, I was unable to eat at all. I would get extremely nervous and anxious, take a few bites, and then usually have to find a restroom as quickly as possible for fear of getting sick.

I remember on one occasion being so afraid of getting on a plane because I didn't want to have a panic attack in the air. I was meeting a young lady and flying across the ocean to meet a friend and do some mission work. I had flown several times before and had never had a problem feeling even the slightest bit nervous, but this time was different. I felt completely terrified. As soon as I got to the gate, I began freaking out, shaking, crying, and feeling physically sick.

I remember calling my husband so that he could talk me through it. He always knew how to get me to calm down. He talked with me and prayed with me. He told me that I was completely fine, that I had to get on the plane and face the fear, that once I was on the plane I would be ok. His advice proved true for me. Once I got on the plane, the fear and anxiety began to subside, and I was, as he said, completely fine.

On a different occasion, I was in a meeting room with no more than twenty students, getting ready to speak. We were leading a small start-up youth group in a young church at the time. The group was small, so it wasn't the number of people that was intimidating. I had spoken many times in the past, so I wasn't intimidated by doing something that was new or hard.

My husband had asked me to share my testimony of how I first became a Christ follower. It was a story I had shared many times. I thought I would be fine getting up in front of the group and sharing how God had changed my life. About five minutes before it was time for me to speak, I got so physically ill, I had to run to the bathroom. Was I coming down with the flu? Did I eat something I shouldn't have? There was no explanation. I couldn't be nervous. I didn't feel nervous. I wouldn't be nervous in front of twenty people sharing something I had shared countless times before. I was completely fine all day. Why was this happening?

I was so sick, I didn't know if I would be able to leave the bathroom. I knew what my options were. I could tell my husband I was too sick to speak, or I could try to gather myself and see if I could make it through my talk. I decided to press through and share my testimony. I was a little shaky, but I felt better as the minutes passed and I made it through. When I was finished, I didn't need to return to the bathroom and I was fine for the rest of the night.

I thought what had happened was extremely odd, and I just hoped that it would never happen again. But, it did. After that night, any time I had the opportunity to speak, I would be so anxious, short of breath, dizzy, and sick to my stomach. I thought that maybe it was just stage fright, just nerves, and that after a few times it would get better, but it didn't.

It got harder and harder for me to speak in front of people and I wasn't sure if I wanted to fight that every time. Not only that, but I wasn't sure if I even could.

CHAPTER 1 PROCESS TIME
What is Happening to Me?

Overcoming an obstacle begins with knowing exactly what you're up against. This section will help you identify specifically what it is you are going to fight. Take your time. It may be difficult to go back through your experience. You may be feeling anxious just writing and reading your thoughts, feelings, and memories. Pray, breathe slowly, and keep going. This is an important part of your journey to healing.

1. Describe your most recent or most memorable encounter with anxiety. Include as many details as possible. Where were you? What were you doing? Who was with you? What was happening in your life during that time? What were you feeling? What thoughts did you have? How did you respond?

2. Now go back and read through your encounter. As you read through your encounter, think of your other encounters with anxiety. How did you feel? How did you respond?

Use the space below to list your common feelings and responses when anxiety arises.

3. How do you think someone without anxiety would feel and respond in the scenario you described?

My hope and prayer for you is that through all you are feeling at this very moment, that you would know you are not alone and that with God's help you can overcome this. I want you to know that you can feel and respond like that person you described in the last question. The person in question #3 is the future you, healthy and free.

I've been there. I know. And I believe in you.

CHAPTER 2
The Search for Answers

I got to the point where I didn't know if I would ever feel better. Would this ever go away? Would I ever go back to normal, whatever normal was anyway? Would I ever come to the point where I didn't feel like a stack of bricks was laying on my chest, restricting my breathing? Would I ever feel comfortable in front of a group of people again? I wanted answers.

Still not completely convinced that the health issues I was experiencing were due to anxiety, I began seeing different doctors to find out what else could be going on with me. I made an appointment with a cardiologist. If I was experiencing dizziness and shortness of breath, I wanted to make sure it wasn't my heart. I wore a monitor for weeks to see if there was any abnormal activity. I was convinced that something was wrong and he was going to find out and tell me so that I could get better. They performed a heart echo and the tests came back. Want to guess what the results were? You guessed it. The results were completely normal. So, the heart doctor gave me two thumbs up, but I wasn't done with my research yet.

I went to see my gynecologist, thinking maybe my

hormone levels were off. With a checkup and some blood work, maybe he would be able to tell me what was going on. He ran tests and couldn't find anything wrong. I remember sitting with my doctor and telling him what was going on with me. I began to cry as I explained how I had panic attacks and felt sick all of the time and I wanted him to tell me what was wrong.

He began asking about my schedule, what all I had going on in my life. At the time, my schedule was completely insane. I was raising small children, working outside of the home, and volunteering in youth groups and leadership meetings almost every night of the week. On top of that, we would travel and minister on the weekends. After I was done telling him all of the things we were involved in, he looked at me and simply said, "Maybe you're just doing too much. You might need to slow down." How could that be? I never felt like I was doing enough to make a difference with my life. I thought that I needed to do more, not less.

At the time, I was not ready to receive that. I could do anything, right? Push myself to my breaking point, all in the name of being a good person, a good enough Christian. If I was living whole-heartedly for the Lord, I wouldn't be having problems with anxiety, right? RIGHT?

I started seeing a chiropractor. I thought that maybe it would help with the massive headaches I was getting. I started getting regular adjustments and taking tons of vitamins that he recommended to me. It seemed to help, but I still wasn't myself. I was anxious and sick a majority of the time. I was sick of being sick. I wanted to feel good. I wanted to feel happy. I wanted to breathe easily and not worry about having a panic attack every time I got into my car.

In the middle of my battle with anxiety, I became pregnant with my third child. I began to feel better. It was amazing. I had very little anxiety. My headaches went away. Yes, this was it! Anxiety free! Thank you Jesus, it was over. I can go tell everyone how Jesus healed my body for real this time! Or, so I thought. But, it wasn't over. Anxiety doesn't just go away, or at least that's not how it happened for me.

While I was pregnant with my third child, my husband accepted a job as a youth pastor in a different state, and we decided that we would move our family across the country after the baby was born. What we didn't know at the time was that after we accepted the job, our beautiful baby girl would be born with a cleft lip and a cleft palate. She would need extra love and care, and it wouldn't be easy.

We moved not even two weeks after our baby was born. I was still feeling ok, just getting adjusted to being a mom to three kids and learning to care for our daughter who needed extra attention, especially with feedings, surgeries, and doctors' appointments. It was a bit of a whirlwind, getting adjusted to caring for our new baby, new city, and new church. For a little while, my anxiety subsided, but it was still there, brewing under the surface.

About three months into our move, I began to experience panic attacks again. I would be driving and all of a sudden, it would be hard to breathe. My throat would feel like it was closing up. I would sweat, shake, and cry, wondering why I felt as if my body was spiraling out of control. Sometimes I would have to pull over the van and tell the kids that mommy was sick and she needed to stop until she felt better. I was so shocked it was back. I thought

I was better. I thought I was healed. I thought life would feel different than this. Why? Why was I still sick?

The doctors' appointments continued. I went in for a checkup. I wanted to get everything checked out, get my blood drawn, maybe receive a different diagnosis, and get on some different medication to make this go away. This was a new doctor in a new place. Surely she could give me a different opinion, a better one. I explained everything that was happening to me with the panic attacks, headaches, and stomach pain. She ordered a CT Scan to find out what was causing the headaches. She found nothing. The CT Scan showed there was absolutely nothing wrong.

I was so frustrated. All of my tests were coming back normal when I felt anything but that. I wanted to know what was causing my ailments. This appointment was different than the others. It was extremely significant in my battle with anxiety. She said something to me that I will never forget.

She was prescribing a different anxiety medication for me so that I could try it and see if it would help.

I asked her what the cure was. I asked, "How do I get better?"

She looked at me and said, "Some people have anxiety and some people don't. You are one of the people who do. But, we can give you something to help you manage it."

I was completely caught off guard. She was basically telling me there wasn't a cure, that I would always have it, that it would be something I would always need to manage. This would be something I would struggle with the rest of my life? It was a moment I will always remember because of what happened next. I felt the Holy Spirit rise up on the inside of me say, "No. That's not true, Sarah. You don't have to live with this." It was so clear that I was certain it was Him speaking to me.

Not sure of what the next step would be, I decided to try the new medication she prescribed. I figured I would give it a shot and see if this would help me manage my anxiety until I could find out what was really going on with me.

I returned back to my normal life, trying to manage everything. One day at church, I was sitting in a meeting room full of new young leaders that we were developing for the church. We were having normal conversation. There was no conflict, no uncomfortable moments, just a rather normal leadership training meeting. All of a sudden, I broke out in a sweat, started shaking, and had to leave the room.

I remember on a different occasion, I was riding in the car with my husband. He was talking to me, but nothing was sinking in and I was having a very difficult time taking part in the conversation. It felt as if my head were in a different place and nothing quite made sense. I was not adjusting well to this new medication at all.

After alternating between the two extremes of the side effects of this medication, I decided to discontinue using it. I also decided, with guidance from the Holy Spirit, to stop seeing that physician and seek out a new one. Her viewpoint was different than what I knew in my spirit, and I knew that I needed to move in the direction that God was calling me.

I still had my original prescription from my very first

panic attack. I decided to reserve that for travel and other times when my anxiety was at its height. I don't believe that medication is a bad thing. I am not anti-meds. I believe that medication can really help. It was very helpful to me in my quest for answers and good health, but in my heart I did not believe that anxiety medication was a long-term solution for me, and I wanted to be free of the medication. I didn't want to depend on medication to make it through the day. I wanted to depend on God.

CHAPTER 2 PROCESS TIME
The Search for Answers

Use the space provided to sketch out a timeline of your battle with anxiety up to this point. Add as much detail as possible. Are there specific encounters that popped into your mind as you were reading through this last chapter? Have there been people who have spoken into your life about anxiety? Positive? Negative? Write it out in timeline form. This will help you see just how much time and effort you have put into finding answers and what feedback you have received from others.

When you have finished, go back and circle the positive feedback, moments of victory, times in your life that you did not experience anxiety, etc. Then, draw an X through the negative feedback, the times of defeat, and any of the times that anxiety ruled.

Through sketching out your timeline, I pray that God would reveal to you any change of direction you need to make in your search for health and a life free from anxiety. Is there someone who speaks negativity over your situation? God might be leading you to set boundaries with that person. Do you have a doctor who is for you? If not, God might be leading you to find a new one. Are you in an unhealthy or toxic relationship, job, or other environment? God might be leading you to make some changes.

Spend some time in prayer and then jot down anything that you think God is speaking to you about your life and the things you need to change. Pray that he would lead you to scripture concerning these decisions and pray that he would lead you to Godly people you can talk to about these changes and who can help you implement them.

CHAPTER 3
The Turning Point: Anxiety Exposed

A distinct moment in my journey to freedom was on a Sunday morning at church. My husband and I were scheduled to make the announcements on stage that day. It was just two services, each spot no more than ten minutes. No big deal, piece of cake, we can do this in our sleep. We got this. No reason to be nervous.

During the worship song right before we were to step onto the stage, I began to panic. My heartrate increased, I felt sick to my stomach, and I felt like my throat was closing up, making it hard to breathe. I was dizzy, shaking, and completely terrified. I turned to my husband and whispered in his ear that I couldn't do this. I went on to tell him that I would need to leave the room before I got sick in front of everyone.

He looked over at me, having been a constant support and encouragement during my three-year-long battle. He kindly, but firmly told me that I was fine, that I was not sick, that there was nothing wrong with me, and that this was just an attack on my destiny. It was fear, and I had to face it. He then told me that I was going to get up on that stage whether I liked it or not.

I became even more terrified knowing that he wasn't going to let me off the hook. I was so shaky and afraid of fainting on the stage. I walked up the stairs, microphone in hand. I had no idea what was about to happen to me. Would I get sick? Would I collapse? Would I even be able to speak?

As I stepped onto the stage and turned around to face the congregation, the panic left immediately. I was completely fine. I was not sick. I did not faint. I stopped shaking. I was able to speak. I was able to do every single thing that I feared I wouldn't be able to do.

I will never forget this defining moment. The Holy Spirit spoke something to me that would propel me even further into my fight for freedom. He said to me, "Even though what you are feeling is very real, your body is responding to a lie." My physical responses were 100% real, but the basis for them was 100% deceit. And if my body was responding negatively based on the lie that there was something physically wrong with me, that there are things I should fear, then how differently might my body respond if I believed the truth of God's Word for my situation?

In that moment on stage, the Holy Spirit confirmed that very thing He spoke to me in the doctor's office. "You can fight this."

CHAPTER 3 PROCESS TIME
The Turning Point: Anxiety Exposed

After reading this chapter, you may have just realized there are lies that have been controlling your life. Or, maybe you have known what that lie is for quite some time, but you just can't shake it. Use the space below to write out any lie the enemy has been speaking over your life, any lie that you have begun to believe as truth. You may only have one. That is ok. Just leave the rest of the space blank. You may have many. That is ok, too. Just take extra space and continue to list them until you feel a sense of peace.

After you have done that, find a scripture that contradicts each lie and write it in the space provided. This is the truth you are going to begin focusing on! Over time, you will no longer believe the lies; you will believe only the truth. And not only that, you will begin to walk in that truth and live that abundant life that Jesus promised to you.

LIE:

TRUTH:

LIE:

TRUTH:

LIE:

TRUTH:

LIE:

TRUTH:

LIE:

TRUTH:

CHAPTER 4
The Fear: Identifying the Root of Anxiety

Anxiety is rooted in fear. I had dealt with fear my entire life, but I had gotten so busy with proving and performing that I neglected looking after my own soul. Instead of dealing with the fear and getting some help, I just plowed ahead with life and ignored my issue. The busyness that I talked about it Chapter 1 was actually a response to my fear of not being good enough.

When we ignore fear in our lives, it doesn't just go away. It grows and it gives birth to anxiety. That anxiety then begins to control every area of our lives and has a negative impact on our overall health and quality of life.

> WHEN WE **IGNORE** FEAR IN OUR LIVES, IT DOESN'T JUST GO AWAY. IT **GROWS** AND IT GIVES BIRTH TO ANXIETY.

I had been afraid for as long as I could remember. As a young girl, I was afraid of someone breaking into our home and hurting us. I would peek under the bed and into the closet, making sure it was safe to get into bed and go to sleep. Most people I've talked to would say this kind of behavior is completely normal, that everyone at some point thinks there is a boogie man under the bed or in the closet, and that we grow out of it as we get older. However, for me, that fear never went away. I was in my 20's, still peeking under the bed and in the closet.

My husband was traveling a good bit, speaking and doing mission work. We loved going together, but there were times I needed to stay home and care for our kids. When I was at home alone at night, I would become so afraid of someone breaking in the house that I would begin acting completely irrational. I was so controlled by fear that I was even afraid of being afraid! During the day, I would tell myself, "Tonight, you will be fine. You're fine during the day in the house. What's the difference at night? You can do it. Tonight's your night." But, when nighttime would come, fear would take over and determine the course of my night. When I knew I was going to have to be alone at night, I would call friends to come stay with me. I felt as if I couldn't be alone. If I couldn't find someone to come over and stay the night with me, I would feel a defeat creep over me, knowing that I would be alone and that I would have a rough night ahead of me.

I would turn all the lights on in the house, turn the

tv on, and lay on the couch paralyzed in fear, refusing to go to sleep. If I could just make it until 4AM or 5AM, when the early risers in the neighborhood ventured out for work, I would be fine. Then I could sleep until the baby woke up and maybe catch a nap sometime in the middle of the day.

This went on for years. I was allowing the enemy to steal something so precious to me during those years, and that was my sleep. I needed sleep so badly as a young mom, but I wasn't getting it when I was at home alone. Even when my husband was at home, I would be afraid of someone breaking in and harming us. I would wake him up frequently and ask him, "Did you hear that? What was that noise?" I could tell he was growing weary of it, that he was having a hard time understanding why I couldn't just go to sleep. He would tell me to just trust God and go to sleep, but I just didn't know how to do that.

Fear had always been a normal way of life for me. Fear of the dark, fear of being hurt, fear of heights, fear of failing, fear of being taken advantage of, fear of what people thought of me, fear of losing control, fear of dying, fear of being a disappointment, and the list goes on. As I grew in my relationship with God, I began to see that a life filled with fear was anything but normal and that I needed to be free.

I had to face the fact that whatever area of life that contained fear was an area in which I did not trust God. Fear manifests itself in different ways, one of which is in people-pleasing. People-pleasing ran my life. I was afraid of letting people down. I would do things for other people, not necessarily because I wanted to, but because I wanted to make them happy and I was afraid I would make them upset if I didn't do what they wanted. I was afraid of rejection. I was afraid of losing them. I was afraid they would think negatively of me. I would do things for people because I felt guilty if I didn't. I didn't want to live like that any longer. I wanted to have relationships that were life-giving, not ones that were rooted in fear.

> **I HAD TO FACE THE FACT THAT WHATEVER AREA OF LIFE THAT CONTAINED FEAR WAS AN AREA IN WHICH I DID NOT TRUST GOD.**

Fear also manifests itself as the fear of not being good enough and the fear of failure. I was extremely insecure. I would walk into a room and feel as if everyone in the room was better than me, as if I didn't belong, as if I could never be as good as other women. As a young mom and minister, I would pour myself into working and trying to prove that I was good enough and that I belonged. I felt guilty having a day go by without doing something that I could consider meaningful. Who was I ministering to that day? What work at home needed to be done? Working is a good thing, and we need to work to make things happen, but fear can drive us over the edge if we are finding our value and worth in what we do. When we are driven by fear, nothing we do is ever enough.

During my battle with anxiety, there were days I thought I would never be free. Living with anxiety is like walking around with a stack of bricks on top you. The anxiety seemed to sit heavily on my chest, making it hard for me to breathe easily, hard for me to relax at all. I was trying to hold my life together, but in the back of my mind I knew that at any moment I could be in a state of panic, unable to control my body's responses.

I was praying for God to take the anxiety away, but I was not dealing with the underlying issue of unresolved fear. I wanted to keep the fear and not the anxiety, and it just doesn't work that way. They both have to go. There is no place for fear or anxiety in an abundant life. I began to realize that if I were to ever be free of anxiety, I would need to face my fears. It was time for me to fight.

I WANTED TO KEEP THE FEAR AND NOT THE ANXIETY, AND IT JUST DOESN'T WORK THAT WAY. THEY BOTH HAVE TO GO.

CHAPTER 4 PROCESS TIME
The Fear: Identifying the Root of Anxiety

In this chapter, I mentioned different fears that I experienced in my life. When you choose to fight, you have to know what you are fighting. Use the space provided to identify your fears. There is no fear too great or too small to be mentioned. If it comes to mind, write it down.

Think back to your most recent encounters with anxiety. Think about what was happening and how you responded. Ask the question, "Where was I? What was happening around me? Why did I respond that way? What was I afraid of?"

Identifying your fears will help you face your fears. With every fear you face, you are digging up a root of your anxiety. How do you get rid of weeds in a garden? Dig them up by the root. That's what you have to do with anxiety. When you dig up the fears, the anxiety withers and dies, leaving more room for that abundant life God has for you.

Below, fill in the blanks until you feel you are done identifying your fears. Be completely honest. If you do not admit having a certain fear, that fear will stay and grow and choke out your joy and peace. This is a time to look your fears in the face and say, "You've been hanging around long enough, but today is the day I tell you to leave. I'm coming for you and I will win."

SETTING: (place, people, situation)

RESPONSE:

FEAR:

SETTING: (place, people, situation)

RESPONSE:

FEAR:

SETTING: (place, people, situation)

RESPONSE:

FEAR:

SETTING: (place, people, situation)

RESPONSE:

FEAR:

SETTING: (place, people, situation)

RESPONSE:

FEAR:

CHAPTER 5

The Fight: The Daily Decision to Take a Stand

Anxiety seemed to just show up one day unannounced, declare itself boss of my life, and dictate every decision of my day. Would I need to drive today? If I did drive, would I be so anxious that I would have a panic attack in line to pick my kids up from school? Would I need to pull over on the side of the road until I could regain control of my responses? Would I get sick or dizzy the next time I spoke in front of others? Would I visibly shake? Would I have to leave the stage? Would I have to walk out of tough meetings because I was too anxious?

Just thinking about my day would cause me to be anxious. I would feel a heaviness in my chest and a lump in my throat. I would tell myself, "Breathe, Sarah. Don't cry. It's going to be ok." Every day, I would face a decision. Do I let anxiety rule over my life, or do I let God rule over my life? Do I live based on what may happen, or do I live based on what God's word has to say? I had to decide whether I would let anxiety beat me up and declare victory over my day, or if I would fight back.

I began to pray that God would lead me in my fight. I began to ask him to guide me through each step of this battle. As I began to seek God for a plan of action, he was faithful to lead me and help me. The Holy Spirit became my advisor.

FIGHTING THE FEAR

Once I discovered that fear was at the root of the anxiety, it was something I could no longer ignore. When anxiety would rise up on the inside of me, I would ask the question, "What am I afraid of right now?" If I was afraid of dying, I would remind myself that I cannot keep myself alive, that only God can do that. If I was afraid of someone harming me, I would remind myself of God's promises that had not yet come to pass, meaning that he wasn't done with me yet. If I was afraid of someone hurting my children or taking them away from me, I would remind myself that I needed to trust God to care for them.

I began to face different fears in my life. I had been afraid of the dark for as long as I could remember. And wouldn't you know, my husband and my kids just love to play hide and seek in the dark. It's my least favorite game because I hate being in the dark, but I knew not playing with them was letting fear control my relationship with my family. So, I reluctantly played with them, and over time it got easier and easier to be in the dark. I know this may seem silly to you, but I hope it can help someone who is reading this. I was always so embarrassed by my fear that I didn't want to admit it to anyone, but the more I faced it and the more I talked about it, the less power it had over me.

WHEN ANXIETY **ATTACKED**, I ATTACKED BACK WITH THE **TRUTH** OF GOD'S WORD.

When I became afraid that someone would break into our home, I would remind myself that all the doors were locked and that being afraid could not control someone else's actions. I would pray God's protection over our home and family and then I would make myself close my eyes and go to sleep. Again, the more I was open about my fear and the more I faced my fear, the easier and easier it became to go to sleep trusting that God was going to take care of us.

I began to face my stage fright by speaking at any opportunity I could. No matter how I felt physically, I would remind myself that there was nothing physically wrong with me and I would force myself to get on stage and speak to people. Again, the more I faced my fear, the easier it became to speak in front of others.

Do I still become afraid? Yes, absolutely. Do I let fear control how I am going to live? No, not anymore.

My fight against anxiety was a fight is every area of my life: spiritually, mentally, emotionally, and physically. If I had neglected one of these areas, I do not believe I would be living free right now.

THE FIGHT IN MY SPIRIT

Just like the enemy can use sin to try to keep us from a full life in Christ, he can use fear to do the same. I could see how the enemy was using anxiety to try to keep me from living out God's purposes and promises for my life. The key word there is TRY. He can try, but he can't succeed when we understand that we can fight him.

Recognizing that God had given me His word as a sword to fight the enemy, I printed out scriptures and placed them under my pillow. I wrote them on my bathroom mirror. I put them on index cards in my purse. I made a note of them in my phone. Any scripture I could latch onto that gave me hope in my fight against anxiety would be within my reach at any given moment of the day. When anxiety attacked, I attacked back with the truth of God's word. Ephesians 6 teaches us that we have armor to wear every day in our fight against the enemy's schemes on our lives.

I WAS ALWAYS SO EMBARRASSED BY MY FEAR THAT I DIDN'T WANT TO ADMIT IT TO ANYONE, BUT THE MORE I FACED IT AND THE MORE I TALKED ABOUT IT, THE LESS POWER IT HAD OVER ME.

"Finally, be strong in the Lord and in his mighty power. Put on the full armor of God, so that you can take your stand against the devil's schemes. For our struggle is not against flesh and blood, but against the rulers, against the authorities, against the powers of this dark world and against the spiritual forces of evil in the heavenly realms. Therefore put on the full armor of God, so that when the day of evil comes, you may be able to stand your ground, and after you have done everything, to stand. Stand firm then, with the belt of truth buckled around your waist, with the breastplate of righteousness in place, and with your feet fitted with the readiness that comes from the gospel of peace. In addition to all this, take up the shield of faith, with which you can extinguish all the flaming arrows of the evil one. Take the helmet of salvation and the sword of the Spirit, which is the word of God." Ephesians 6:10-17

As you read through the pieces of armor, every piece is defensive except for one. They are all meant to protect us against the attacks of the enemy, except for one. The only offensive weapon God has given to us is the sword of the spirit, which is the Word of God.

The Bible is our only weapon, yet we can sometimes neglect to fully apply its words to our life simply because we have prayed about something. "Well, I prayed that I wouldn't have anxiety anymore, and it's still here. I guess when God's ready to take it from me, he will. Until then, I'll just be miserable I guess." Friend, NO! We have the Word of God to speak over our lives and to use in our fight against the enemy so that we can walk in victory.

Over our lifetime, different seeds are planted by people, the enemy, and our life experiences. Seeds of fear had been planted in my soul, and they grew over time into a life-crippling anxiety.

Hebrews 4:12 says, "For the word of God is alive and active. Sharper than any double-edged sword, it penetrates even to dividing soul and spirit, joints and marrow; it judges the thoughts and attitudes of the heart."

When we speak God's Word over our lives, seeds are planted into our souls. When we plant scriptures into our souls, they grow and produce life. When we have God's Word growing in us, it will choke out the weeds sent from the enemy. You may not see a difference right away, but over time you will notice the scriptures you planted in your soul are giving life to the areas that were once hurting and dying.

I began to notice that what was going on in my life contradicted the words I was reading in my Bible. I was anxious about EVERYTHING, yet Philippians 4:6-7 says, "Do not be anxious about ANYTHING, but in every situation, by prayer and petition, with thanksgiving, present your requests to God. And the peace of God, which transcends all understanding, will guard your hearts and your minds in Christ Jesus."

The word of God was not only telling me that I didn't have to be anxious, but that I shouldn't be. "DO NOT be anxious." If God was telling me through his word to not be anxious, then it must be possible for me to live without anxiety. I knew him enough to know that he was not asking something of me that was impossible for me to accomplish.

IF GOD WAS TELLING ME THROUGH HIS WORD TO NOT BE ANXIOUS, THEN IT MUST BE POSSIBLE FOR ME TO LIVE WITHOUT ANXIETY.

1 Peter 5:7 says, "Cast all your anxiety on him because he cares for you."

Again, God was telling me that I didn't have to carry my anxiety around, that I could give it to him, and that I should give it to him.

It was encouraging to me to have scriptures to lean on during my battle with anxiety because each of them reminded me that my battle would not go on forever, that it would end, and that with God's help, I would overcome. So, I began declaring these scriptures over my life. I wrote them down and put them in places where I could see them multiple times a day. I would pray over them and think about them. I would bring those promises in scripture to the Lord in my prayer time. "God, you said this, and I believe it. Make it so in my life."

THE FIGHT IN MY MIND AND EMOTIONS

Our decisions begin in our mind. What you think is who you will be. How you think is how you will live. If your mind is filled with fear and anxiety, your life will be filled with it as well.

WHAT YOU THINK IS WHO YOU WILL **BE**. HOW YOU THINK IS HOW YOU WILL **LIVE**.

1 Corinthians 2:16 tells us that we have the mind of Christ. Christ made some really courageous choices in his life here on earth. And since our actions begin in our mind and we have the mind of Christ, we can have thoughts like

his that will lead to actions like his. Because fear and anxiety did not rule over the thoughts and actions of Christ, they do not have to rule over mine either.

It's important to evaluate what thoughts are running through our minds and what we have been feeding our minds. In my fight with anxiety, I had to ask myself some honest questions. Are my thoughts positive or negative? Do I believe in myself, or do I doubt myself? Is my mind filled with faith or with fear? Am I dreaming of what God could do, or am I waiting for something bad to happen? Am I listening to music that is good for my thought life, or is it detrimental to my thinking patterns? Am I watching and reading things that are causing my mind to think on what is good, or on what will cause destruction in my life?

When you begin to ask questions like that, God will begin to shine his light on the parts of your life you can change in order to feed your mind what it needs to thrive and not to fret. When you change what goes in your mind, your thoughts will change as well. When you begin to fill your mind with music, books, podcasts, and conversations that are life-giving, you will have more life-giving thoughts. And when you have life-giving thoughts, you will have life-giving actions.

Emotional health is vital to living a life free from anxiety's control. Anxiety breeds on unresolved emotional hurts. During my fight with anxiety, it came to my attention that I had unforgiveness and unresolved hurts in my life. Hurts from my childhood, hurts from my teen years, and hurts as an adult. I prayed that I would be healed. I talked about it with my husband and sometimes a close friend. I read what the Bible had to say about forgiveness. I read books about forgiveness. I desperately wanted to forgive, but for some reason I couldn't shake it. I couldn't get free and I didn't know why. I decided to go to a counselor and open up about what was going on. He didn't give me five ways to get free or a book on how to forgive. He just listened to me. And for the first time in a long time, I felt like my feelings were justified, like it was ok to feel the way I felt.

It is important to forgive and release others. It is important to forgive and release yourself. I was carrying around way too much, and it didn't all fit in my heart and in my mind. I was pushing all of my feelings down and not dealing with them, and they grew and began to choke out any trace of emotional well-being. I had to release my feelings and know that it was ok to do that.

Acknowledging how I was feeling and allowing myself to feel that way were huge steps in my recovery. I was being way too hard on people and way too hard on myself. I was bottling emotions inside because I didn't feel like I had a safe space to open up.

When you feel that way, counseling can be a great place to turn. Pastors, mentors, and close friends are there to help you as well. God never meant for us to walk through battles alone. He has gifted people with the ability to listen and give wisdom and insight to help us get emotionally healthy. Once I laid down my pride and my fear of being rejected, I began to heal.

Many times, we seek justification for how we are feeling from the people who hurt us. Most of the time... ok, 99.99999% of the time, you will not receive justification from the person who hurt you. You may or may not receive an apology. You may or may not see changed behavior. In fact, having that person say, "It is absolutely, perfectly ok for you to feel that way" is probably not going to happen.

The good news is that we are justified through a relationship with Jesus Christ. We don't need to seek justification for our feelings from people. In the face of conflict, each person involved is biased toward their own perspective of the situation-- everyone except for Jesus. He is not biased; He is just. Jesus makes the wrong things right. He ministers healing and wholeness to our hearts, no matter what we have been through. You don't need anyone but him to tell you that it is ok to feel the way you are feeling.

If you can relate to the things I'm sharing in this section, I highly encourage you to see a Christian counselor. Wounds, unforgiveness, and bitterness are enemies to our emotional health. We don't have to let them have control over our lives. With God's help, we can

> YOU DON'T NEED ANYONE BUT HIM TO TELL YOU THAT IT IS OK TO **FEEL** THE WAY YOU ARE **FEELING**.

get emotionally free.

Find a safe place and safe people so that you can be honest and real about what you are feeling. Don't let your fear of being found out keep you from your freedom.

THE FIGHT IN MY BODY

It's not fun when your body is freaking out and you can't figure out why. I was so tired of feeling bad. I began to seek out natural alternatives to medicine to handle my anxiety. I began to research anxiety and what caused it and how I could get better.

In my research, I read that anxiety is at its height when you are low on sleep, so I began to get more sleep. At the beginning of my fight, if I got less than seven hours of sleep, I was a mess. Eight hours is the goal!

One thing that helped me tremendously in my fight against anxiety was the knowledge of essential oils. I began to use certain oils to help calm me down. I took them everywhere with me. Don't worry, I'm not going to try to sell you oils or recruit you to a team. But I can't talk about the physical fight without mentioning essential oils. A couple of friends introduced me to oils, and it was monumental in my fight. If I started to have a panic attack while I was driving, I would open up a calming oil and within a couple of minutes I was calmer. It can take some time to find the oil that works for you, but it really did work for me, and it's natural with no side effects.

I also read that panic attacks were most common when you are under stress and that exercise releases stress. I was in prayer one day and was led by the Holy Spirt to begin running. Now, when I tell people that, they tell me that there is no way they could be a runner. While it is good news that running is not the only exercise that can release stress, it's the type of exercise that I was led to try. At this point in life, I was unable to even run half of a mile without feeling completely winded and useless. However, at the same time God was speaking to me to run, my oldest daughter joined a running group at her school and needed help training for a 5K. God has an incredible sense of humor, doesn't he? As I began running with my daughter to push and train her, I was also being pushed and trained. We did a couple of 5K's together, and I completed a 10K trail run. A half marathon is next on my list!

However, it did not come easy. I just knew what God had spoken to me and I pushed myself to go a little further each time I ran. The more I ran, the better I felt, not during the actual running, of course, but in the days to follow. The running was enough exertion to get rid of any stress from my daily responsibilities. I began to decide if I would run or not depending on whether I wanted to feel good that day or not. I decided to run more often than not, and my anxiety began to lower.

At this point in my journey, I was on a day by day, touch and go basis. Some days I felt good, some days I didn't. I was free from any medication, and my level of anxiety was dependent upon my level of self-care, something I was learning to do and not feel guilty about. I could tell I was getting better, but I wasn't there yet.

Over time, the anxiety began to break. One day I realized that I hadn't had a panic attack in quite some time. Sometimes we pray to be healed and then we get confused or upset when the healing doesn't come. I have been in that place before. God can heal instantaneously. I see it in my Bible, and I've seen it up close and personal. However, that is not how he healed me of anxiety. He still healed me, it just wasn't the way I thought he would. He took me on a journey to find the root and he coached me on my journey to health and wholeness.

CHAPTER 5 PROCESS TIME

The Fight: The Daily Decision to Take a Stand

Use the space below to write out a plan of action for your fight against anxiety toward a life of health and wholeness. We know that we need to fight if we are going to be free, the question is, "How are we going to fight?" Decide what practical actions need to be taken to care for yourself in the following areas.

MY SPIRIT:

MY MIND AND MY EMOTIONS:

MY BODY:

CHAPTER 6

The Freedom: How to Walk It Out

When I first received prayer to be free from anxiety, a young lady told me that one day I would wake up and the anxiety would be gone and the panic attacks would just cease. It wasn't until about four years later when that happened, but it did. My freedom didn't come right away, and it didn't come the way I thought it would. But, even though the word she spoke over me didn't happen the way I thought it would, it did come to pass. God is good at keeping His promises. I just had to believe that I could be free, that He would deliver me like He said He would. It was a daily fight, but that day did come when I just didn't battle with it anymore.

In the midst of my battle with anxiety, I felt as if I would never feel like myself again. I thought that how I felt was how I would always feel. I felt as if I would be bound forever. But, God's truth and his promises for our lives are so much greater than anything that we feel.

I was better. I could get on stage without getting sick or freaked out. I could lay my head down at night without feeling like it would be my last. I no longer looked in closets or under beds. I could get on an airplane with confidence in God to protect me. I could drive for long distances without having a panic attack. I could meet with strong leaders and eat in nice restaurants without feeling intimidated or like I didn't belong.

God did it. He set me free. He had a much better life for me than I ever dreamed. He didn't want me to be controlled by fear, people-pleasing, performance, or guilt. He didn't want me to live panicked and freaked out all of the time. He wanted me to live a life of freedom in Him.

John 10:10 (NASB) says, "The thief comes only to steal and kill and destroy; I came that they may have life, and have it abundantly."

A life controlled by fear and anxiety is no life at all. Jesus came to give us a full life, a life that we could enjoy. We only have to believe that we can have a life like that. Just like it took faith for me to be saved and to come into a relationship with God through his son Jesus Christ, it took faith for me to know I could live a life without anxiety.

My health is still something I have to really focus on to live in freedom. I need exercise. I need to eat

JUST LIKE IT TOOK **FAITH** FOR ME TO BE SAVED AND TO COME INTO A RELATIONSHIP WITH GOD THROUGH HIS SON JESUS CHRIST, IT TOOK FAITH FOR ME TO **KNOW** I COULD LIVE A LIFE WITHOUT ANXIETY. well. I need plenty of rest. I need to be mindful of the amount of stress I have in my life. I need healthy relationships. I need consistent time with God in prayer and Bible study. I have to stay filled up. I no longer completely and repetitively empty myself. When I pour myself out for others, I go and get filled back up. It's very important that I care for myself so that I can live that abundant life God promised me in His word, and so that it can spill out onto others.

Does anxiety try to creep back into my life? Yes, it does. It TRIES. But once the lies of the enemy were exposed in that area of my life, it was no longer an option for me to let him take the joy out of my life. When I feel anxious, I pray and I tell the enemy that he will not win. I speak scripture over myself. And I evaluate my life to see where I need to better care for myself.

It tries to sneak back in every once in a while, but it quickly leaves because I know it's a lie and a trick. Just like I remind myself that I am free from my past sins whenever I feel tempted, I remind myself of how God freed me from anxiety and that I'm not going back to a life of constant worry and misery. A life of freedom is much better that a life bound by fear.

So, if that anxiety comes knocking on your door, tell it you're home but you're not answering the door, and lock that top lock and go about your business. It will leave. I promise you it will. God promises you it will. James 4:7 says, "Submit yourselves, then, to God. Resist the devil, and he will flee from you." Once you are healthy and free, the enemy will present opportunities for you to become afraid or to worry, but it is an opportunity that you no longer have to accept.

When I was battling anxiety, I didn't know I would write about it. I knew that God was calling me to write, but I didn't know what he wanted me to write about. Many times during the battle, I would ask

God, "Why are you allowing me to go through this? Why is this part of my life? You can do anything, so why won't you just take this from me?"

I didn't understand why I had to fight it, why I wasn't instantaneously healed and delivered, but now I better understand why God allowed me to journey, to fight, to overcome. Overcoming anxiety is now a testimony that I can share with others. I now have a story to write and give to others.

Before I began writing this, I began to share publicly that I had fought anxiety and that with God, I had won. I had several people approach me asking me how they too could be free. They had tried everything. Why were they bound? Why couldn't they shake it? They wanted me to help them, but I found it difficult to do that in one sitting. I found it difficult to put into conversational words how I became free. I knew I needed to put it on paper.

I pray that reading my story has encouraged you. I pray that there is a hope that is stirring on the inside of you. I pray that there is a longing and an urgency to be free. I pray that God is revealing to you what steps to take as you begin your journey to freedom. And I pray that you would now know that you are not alone and that it is possible to live free from the bondage of anxiety.

CHAPTER 6 PROCESS TIME
The Freedom: How to Walk It Out

Use the space provided to write a prayer. Express your thoughts and desires to God and thank him in advance for all he is going to do in your life. Be as specific as possible so that you can refer back to this prayer and see what he has done for you in your journey to freedom.